FamilyPreneur: The Six Key Steps to
Raising Your Little Entrepreneurs
By Jean Pierre Rukebesha,
©WorkBook Press , 2020

ISBN: *978-1-954753-15-0 (Paperback Version)*
                 978-1-952754-19-7 (Digital Version)

WorkBook
PRESS

FAMILYPRENEUR

PRENEUR

The Six Key Steps to Raising
Your Little Enrepreneurs

JEAN PIERRE RUKEBESHA

CONTENTS

CONTENTS

CONTENTS

CHAPTER ONE

The Challenge

The Six Key Steps to Raising Your Little Entrepreneur

More likely than not, if you're reading this book, you are, most likely, both an entrepreneur and a parent. You are also probably wondering how best to get your children interested in following in your footsteps. Here are a number of additional questions you might be asking :

> What is a good age to start introducing my child (or children) to the concept of entrepreneurship in general and then in my business, specifically?

> What can I be doing to involve my child (or children) on a daily, weekly and monthly basis in my company?

> How can I make learning about my business interesting and even fun for my kids?

In this book, I'll share with you the answers to the above questions and many others.

Entrepreneurship is, indeed, one of the best ways of ensuring income for a family. We are also aware that much of the information we receive through the media, daily, is about big corporations Yet many of us know the truth that the economy of any country, to be successful, is based on a successful, functioning small businesses. These make up a significant chunk of the revenue-generating from any country, for tax purposes, for building families' income and worth, et cetera.

It also goes without saying that the government of any country will never be able to employ everybody. Many countries abandoned the central planning economies, which were terrible in a way that resources were not being utilized to the optimum because of various reasons. Everybody has been getting away from centralized economies to a free market, where people can be free to think and try and experiment with different ways of how they can be more efficient – which is the foundation of capitalism.

Having said that, not everybody is going to work for bigger corporations. If you look at larger businesses, employees put into a kind of a box where, in most cases, their creative minds will be stifled. They will not be allowed to do what they would like to do. They will not experiment. They will not even benefit if they come up with great ideas. That's where entrepreneurship is very, very important. As one entrepreneurial expert I know has stated,

"Entrepreneurship is whereare creativity lies and where our hope is."

One of the classic examples I give starts with the following. Suppose a child takes over a family business that has been around for 10-15 years. Their mom and dad have done all they could to stabilize the company. Sure, they might have had struggles in the beginning, but in the end, they might find they would have been able to guarantee themselves a five-figure salary every year with all the flexibilities. Yes, they have to work hard, but they did.

Now, imagine their children starting to work in the family business at the age, of, say eight. They don't do much but they get acquainted with things like the lay of the land inside the office or factory. They also are acknowledged by the other workers as contributors to the company's bottom line. Additionally, whether they realize it or not, they are geting introduced to the things that make a business tick—the marketing, the operations, the financial function, management processes and so forth. By the time they hit 18 or after they finish college, they are fully equipped to take over some or most of the functions of the business. These "prepared children" could easily go from young kids working with their parents when they finish high school or college, from, let's say, a salary of $30,000 to $100,000 within three to four years. This outcome depends on how quickly they catch up with understanding the business and being able to operate it, but this jump in salary has been proven to be feasible for many familypreneurial companies.

Other types of businesses can't create similar opportunities. No matter how much someone is qualified, the rapid payment ramp-up is not possible with a traditional corporate work path. When a child takes over the family business, he or she boosts the economy because the company involved doesn't die. Instead, through the transference of ownership, the company can, instead, accelerate its growth, bringing new opportunities and jobs to the community. The child who has taken over can has the assets of the company that can be leveraged. There is no question that building up an existing business is a more prudent choice. The above are just a few of the reasons I believe small business succession planning, especially family-business succession planning, should be given high attention. Yes, individually, these companies don't make a tremendous amount of money, which means they don't get the publicity they should get. But, we know that, in an aggregate, if you address them as an collective of highpotential businesses, they end up creating a huge machine that, frankly, runs the economy.

In provinces, like Alberta, Canada where we have about 150,000 registered businesses, around 96% of them are considered to be "small companies." They employ between one to five people. The other 4% is what we call "big business." And it's these businesses are the ones that get the lion's share of publicity. Yet the smaller businesses are made up of a lot of families that depend on them, but they don't get the same publicity and community recognition. In other words, they are not valued nor leveraged for the highpotential value they hold.

Again, if you look at what these organizations pay in taxes, you will see they are contributing some of the highest taxes in the economy. If we can help them survive, then their kids or other family members they may bring into the business, won't have to wonder where they will be getting a job or building their career. Instead, they can benefit from learning the trade from inside their family businesses. For each child of entrepreneurial parents that follows this path into the family business, that's one less unemployed person. Further, there is a definite leverage that keeping a business going will create when a business continues beyond the original owner. Here, the base of clients or customers are able to grow even more trust in a business that lives beyond its founders.

It's in this entrepreneurial space that you have, what I would call, a great equalizer. The possibilities of succeeding are unlimited. This refocusing on leveraging family businesses through successions, levels the playing field dramatically.

But what often happens is that when parents start a business, in the beginning, they are struggling. They don't have enough time with their family. They are spending so many hours at work that they miss many opportunities to connect with their kids and share with them what they do. Even though the kids can see the benefit of pop's and mom's hard work because their always eat well or take yearly vacations or they own a beautiful house, it's very hard to connect the two. They are often spoiled children, unaware as to what makes their life so comfortable.

Then, by the time the business has become viable, allowing them to cover recurring family expenses, they might have lost the bond they have with their children. All their kids remember is the struggle, the hard work of the parents at the beginning. At the same time, parents are struggling to get the best life for their kids, so the first thing they do is help them with their education. But they forget that where they are has been a result of the business they built from the ground up through their struggles.

CONNECTING THE BUSINESS TO THE EDUCATIONAL DEVELOPMENT OF YOUR CHILDREN

Now, for some reason, most parents will insist on their kids getting an excellent education, but they don't connect this to the business that they are involved in. So, often, their children end up going to good schools, getting good grades and, then, all of a sudden they start dreaming of joining some of the biggest companies out there that we hear about on TV and radio. This route becomes a norm for many children of family-owned businesses. It's about social status. It's cliché, but often their children will say something like,

"I have to work for my family. What a pain. "

So they stay at your company until maybe they land a job in the field they studied in college or where one of their friends work. They take that job, thinking they will be on the path to a great career—that they will be the exception and climb the corporate ladder faster than those who went before them. But then the years pass and these kids find themselves moving past the age of 30. They begin to realize the road to the top is not as easy as they thought. Just like those who went before them, it's going to take years and years to be able to reach the position or positions that they dreamed they would reach before 40.

By this time, their parents are older and because they have been unable to keep up their stamina, the business they put so much heart and sweat equity into, has declined drastically, leaving a shrunken customer base, piling debts and low morale among any employees still remaining. Then inefficiency creeps in, and all of a sudden, their business is down the drain. A second scenario is that their parents have already given up on leaving the business to anybody, to their siblings or their relatives.

This was the story of one of my clients, I'll call Ken. He has six children—most of them, engineers. Ken built a strong business that was generating a million dollars a year and then expanded it into a successful welding business. From there, he grew his net worth with a lot of good investments.

But, as the years went by, Ken grew weaker and more and more sickly. He couldn't keep up with the demands of his company. He couldn't serve his customers. Right now, sadly, we are liquidating the company slowly, disposing of the assets until we will just shut down the company. This business was worth a million in revenue generated every year. It's now going up in smoke because no one will take over.

Now let's look at a different outcome with another client, I'll call Frank, who has also built a good business. Frank's company is in the sewage/cleaning area. It's not a glamorous job, but it makes him about $800,000 a year. From the outside, nobody would guess that his company does so well.

His son, I'll call Andrew, was training to be a geologist. It happened that by the time he was trying to join a big company in his industry, one of these dream companies he wanted, found the entry point difficult to break in, but he made it. However, very soon after Andrew started at a company in the industry, he was told that it would take at least five years for him to qualify as a geologist along with those five-figure numbers he had always dreamed of making.

When Andrew shared his disappointment with his father, Frank said, "Why don't you come and try working for me? I can pay you that five-figure amount you want to earn right now rather than you having to wait five years." Andrew took up his dad on his offer and left his current employer. Today, he's happier than any other kid I have ever seen. He's earning more money than his older brother who took a traditional corporate career path, plus he has a very flexible work schedule that allows him to take plenty of fourday, mini vacations, enjoying his young life on a daily basis rather than waiting for one or two weeks of vacation a year. You might be thinking, "What a minute. How do I know that my children will even want to go into my business?" To this point, I'll just suggest that you consider opening up the option of teaching your children about your business and involving them, slowly and creatively into your work life.

To this end, nothing will work better than talking with them regularly about your business and, specifically, using the fun tools and ideas that I will share throughout this book to build strong interest in your business. The path to success in raising your little entrepreneurs involves trying different strategies and tactics to see what works best for you and your kids. Your approach will involve gradually introducing your children into your business and slowly get them to appreciate and understand it.

Many business people were kids who started young in their entrepreneurial pursuits. Whether they delivered newspapers door to door in their neighborhood, or sold little things on the street around their house, or even invented something like twelve year-old founder of Mo's Bows, Moziah Bridges, who created cool bow ties for both kids and adults. Moziah, was funded by Damond John from Shark Tank, the very successful show, Shark Tank. Why do those kids end up being successful? Because they were able to connect the dots at a younger age, they were able to appreciate the life of the entrepreneur and get through the fundamentals.

When entrepreneurs talk about their businesses, they often share their processes or philosophies that have worked for them over the years. But, if you were part of a family that started involving you in your parents' business at a young age, you would have an even richer, more colorful and even, perhaps more engaging, story to tell.

It's scary to try to start a company when you've been working in a traditional business for a decade or more, But when people are laid off from work, they struggle, and they don't know what to do. They're scared of taking on the responsibilities of being an entrepreneur because they've never been introduced into an entrepreneurial environment and so they have no idea how to start.

Yet, imagine if your kids had been introduced to the world of entrepreneurship starting when they were in grade school and then running through to their graduation from college? By teaching the basics of entrepreneurship, you can help your children build the essential business and life skills that will serve them throughout their lives. Of course, schools should complement this learning. Just as we teach literacy, mathematics, and history, we should teach business creation and entrepreneurship to them early and keep them connected to learning more about business on an ongoing basis. We don't see these studies offered anywhere in any elementary education, but, there's always tomorrow and as the world becomes more and more aware of the benefits of entrepreneurship, I think we will see changes coming our way sooner than later.

But nothing takes the place of bringing learning into your own home. To this end, I'll share with you a wide variety of tools, techniques and strategies to connect with your kids today and start seeing results within weeks. It is possible!

CHAPTER-BY-CHAPTER OVERVIEW

Following is an outline of the upcoming chapters with a summary each:

CHAPTER 2: STEP 1 EMBRACE YOUR FAMILYPRENEURSHIP HERITAGE FROM YOUR PARENTS

This chapter helps you by providing an overview of past entrepreneurs who had children they inspired to follow them into their businesses. You will also find strategies to build a welcoming entrepreneurial environment into your home. The chapter ends with a variety of activities you can start implementing daily that will engage your kids in fun activities for them to engage in building the interest in entrepreneurship.

CHAPTER 3: STEP 2 TAP INTO YOUR DREAMS TO BUILD THEIR DREAMS

The important thing is to realize that you can lead the change and get started as soon as tomorrow by, first, tapping into your dreams that you had to become an entrepreneur. This is Step 2, where your passion will inspire their passion. Again, this chapter is rich with a wide variety of resources and exercises you can use to get your child inspired.

CHAPTER 4: STEP 3 PREPARE YOUR YOUNG FAMILYPRENEUR

Once you have ignited a passion for entrepreneurship in your child, it's time to address the practical elements and skills he or she will need to move toward the goal of taking over your business one day. From developing management skills to finance skills and more, this chapter will provide you with the tools you need to accomplish this necessary step.

CHAPTER 5: STEP 4 INVOLVE YOUR CHILD IN YOUR BUSINESS TO GAIN THE FAMILYPRENEUR PERSPECTIVE

This chapter shows you how to involve your child directly into your business. It's about slowly giving them activities to experience both your daily work life and the bigger picture that includes your customers or clients, the community where you work and your future plans for growth.

CHAPTER 6: STEP 5 BUILD YOUR CHILD'S BUSINESS KNOWLEDGE

The next step is to build out the infrastructure for your child to start down the path to take over your business. Knowing this, your child can confidently grow into that young man or woman you will be proud to take over the leadership of your company.

CHAPTER 7: STEP 6: EVALUATE YOUR FAMILYPRENEUR SUCCESS

Finally, this chapter focuses on the next level of acclimating your children into your business. Here, it's all about inspecting what you expect. By this I mean creating tools that will help you assess how your child is doing at each milestone on his or her path regarding believing, practicing and developing the rich skills of entrepreneurship.

THE JOURNEY

Note the saying, "The journey of 1000 miles begins with the first step." This was stated by Lao Tzu, the philosopher who is credited with writing the sacred text, "Daodejing." This journey you will be taking that may seem very long, will actually be shorter than you think. This is because the information I will provide you will help you prepare and move, even joyfully, down the entire path to having your child (or children) get involved in your business and, one day, take it over.

"Many of life's failures are people who did not realize how close they were to success when they gave up."

Thomas Edison

CHAPTER TWO

Step one

Embrace Your FamilyPreneurship
Heritage From Your Parents

One of the most famous entrepreneurs in history, Thomas Edison, patented 1,093 inventions during his lifetime. Among them were the light bulb, the early motion picture camera and the phonograph. It was on the significance of those inventions that he built a business empire. Having left school early, Edison took odd jobs selling newspapers and candy. He educated himself by reading everything he could get his hands on to feed his insatiable curiosity about the world. The more he learned, the more he developed a style of thinking that can be characterized in two words. "*What if…?*"

In everything he did, Edison never saw or used a machine he didn't think he could improve, from stock tickers to voting machines to automobile batteries. Reputed to be a tyrant to those who worked for him, he was notorious for relentless experimentation. He would not rest until he knew he got it right. "Many of life's failures are people who did not realize how close they were to success when they gave up," he once said. He also said, "I have not failed. I've just found 10,000 ways that won't work."

Edison was married twice and had six children, three with each wife. Two of his children followed in their father's footsteps to some extent. For example, Charles, his oldest son from his second wife, was the most successful of all the Edison children. He became president of his father's company at age 37 and remained in that post until the company was sold in 1959. But Charles is more well-known for his second career in politics, having served as Assistant Secretary of the Navy under President Franklin Roosevelt and later, he was elected governor of New Jersey. Clearly, there was an interest in his father's work but not enough to keep the business in the family.

Yet, Edison's youngest son, Theodore, was just the type of child parents would love to nurture into following in their footsteps. He was the child most like his father. The family referred to him as "the little laboratory assistant"[1] because of his interest in conducting experiments as a young boy. This endeared him to Edison, but also made him anxious. "Theodore is a good boy," He once said of his son, "but his forte is mathematics. I am a little afraid…he may go flying off into the clouds with that fellow Einstein. And if he does…I'm afraid he won't work with me."[2]

1 https://www.nps.gov/edis/index.htm
2 https://www.nps.gov/edis/index.htm

Theodore went on to graduate with a degree in physics from MIT becoming the only Edison child to finish college. Then he did work with his father successfully. He spent years working with him in various capacities until he built his own laboratory and formed his own company. During his career he obtained more than 80 patents for his own inventions.

Then there was Edison's daughter Madeleine. She was said to have been of a higher intelligence with an aptitude for engineering and science. It's been speculated that if she had been born later, in era where women were more accepted in scientific fields, she may have pursued her father's work as well. But Madeleine and her siblings either showed little interest in following in their father's footsteps or weren't capable of it. Edison even described his oldest son Thomas Jr. as "absolutely illiterate scientifically and otherwise."[3]

Yet, if Edison had mixed results in encouraging his offspring to follow his dream, Henry Ford had much better success.

Like Edison, Ford had a different way of viewing the world. At 13 years old, upon receiving a pocket watch for his birthday, the first thing he did was take it apart. It was that innate desire for knowledge of how things worked that drove Ford throughout his life and his establishment of The Ford Motor Company. He was not an inventor as much as he was an innovator. He believed not just in ideas, but in the efficient execution of those ideas. He took something that already existed, re-engineered it to perform better and resold it as something new. He may not have been the first to build an automobile, but he became the best at manufacturing and selling them. His assembly lines consistently fulfilled his great vision for "a better, cheaper motorcar for the great multitude."[4]

Ford made cars affordable for ordinary Americans and he did it without cutting corners. "Quality means doing it right when no one is looking," he said.

3 http://www.edisonmuseum.org/content8625.html?pageCatID=2
4 https://www.thehenryford.org/explore/stories-of-innovation/visionaries/henry-ford/

He had just one child, a son Edsel, who eventually became president of his father's company for over twenty years. But the entrepreneurial legacy didn't stop there. Edsel's son, Henry Ford II, also went into the business of car manufacturing. He served as president of the company for 15 years until it became a publiclytraded corporation in 1956. Though Henry II can be credited with keeping the company in the family through the third generation, his tenure as head of the company received mixed reviews. After the company went public, he remained as CEO and Chairman and was known for an aggressive, erratic management style until he finally stepped aside in 1982. But the family maintains a strong leadership presence in the company, even in 2016. They now own less than 2% of stock, but hold a permanent controlling interest with 40% of the voting power. Bill Ford, Jr, great-grandson of Henry Ford, has served as executive chairman since 2006 and now there is a fifth generation coming of age.

In 2006, 26-year old Henry Ford III joined his great-greatgrandfather's company and in ten years has spent time in all facets

"Quality means doing it right when no one is looking."

Henry Ford

of the business—product planning, marketing, dealer relations, union negotiation and even spent a summer at a dealership as a salesman. "In the back of my mind, I knew I always wanted to work for Ford," he told the Automotive News in 2014. "Our family's legacy and heritage are very important to me and I knew it was something I wanted to carry on…I truly view myself as just another Ford employee."[5]

The Ford Motor Company may be the most vivid and successful example of an entrepreneurial venture that began with one man's passion and grew to become a thriving family business on a global scale spanning multiple generations. But Henry Ford's first automobile rolled off the assembly line over 100 years ago. Things have changed a bit since then.

Both Edison and Ford lived in an era that produced the foundation for our modern world economy. It's now technology that drives innovation and perhaps no single person has done more to advance the course of technology to change the world than Steve Jobs. Jobs' personality and approach to his work was much more aligned with that of Edison and Ford than his contemporaries. The modern CEO is focused on market share, the company's stock price, and incremental growth. But Jobs' was more interested in changing the way people communicated, worked and lived.

Since his death in 2011, stories of Jobs' relentless passion, arrogance and rebellious nature have become ubiquitous—his habit of walking barefoot in public places, his penchant for berating employees, colleagues, journalists, and even his closest friends. He marched to his own drumbeat and didn't adhere to the polite norms of social engagement. In his 2005 Commencement Address to Stanford University graduates, Jobs famously said "Your time is limited, so don't waste it living someone else's life. Don't be trapped by dogma – which is living with the results of other people's thinking. Don't let the noise of others opinions drown out your own inner voice. And most important, have the courage to follow your heart and intuition. They somehow already know what you truly want to become. Everything else is secondary."

5 http://www.autonews.com/article/20140407/UNDER4001/304079967/henry-ford-iii

Jobs clashed with almost everyone he ever worked with but he never wavered on one point; his insistence that his vision was the correct one and he fought for it every day of his life. About entrepreneurship, Jobs once told an interviewer, "I'm convinced that about half of what separates successful entrepreneurs from the non-successful ones is pure perseverance."

Jobs had four children, and although three of them are still fairly young, none of them have shown a public interest in technology or working for Apple. In fact, Jobs once told the New York Times that he discouraged his children from using technology at all.[6]

Imagine Ford refusing to allow his children to ride in cars or Edison forbidding use of electricity at home. Jobs clearly wasn't interested in grooming his children as successors, but it remains to be seen whether Apple, without his unique passion, tenacity,

6 http://www.nytimes.com/2014/09/11/fashion/steve-jobs-apple-was-a-low-tech-parent.html

"I'm convinced that about half of what separates successful entrepreneurs from the non-successful ones is pure perseverance."

Steve Jobs

and vision, can maintain its unprecedented winning streak of innovation.

PASSING DOWN THE ENTREPRENEURIAL SPIRIT

There are dozens of studies that have attempted to determine the common characteristics of successful entrepreneurs, and even in the stories of Edison, Ford, and Jobs we can clearly see a pattern of some key traits that all successful entrepreneurs have, regardless of race, gender, or the challenges of the era in which they lived. They show the following:

TENACITY

- Jobs called it "pure perseverance," but none of these people gave up. Ever. Their dreams drove them until they achieved everything they envisioned.

PASSION

- It is a love for the work that drives people to work the necessary hours, endure the inevitable failures and deflect the ever-present criticism to stay focused on what they want.

TOLERANCE OF AMBIGUITY

- There is no roadmap. Every entrepreneur's path is unique. The very nature of doing something new and different is that the next step is never clear. Hall of Fame hockey player Wayne Gretzky once said, "I skate to where the puck is going to be, not to where it's been."

VISION

- Henry David Thoreau could have had entrepreneurs in mind when he wrote, "It's not what you look at that matters, it's what you see."

SELF—BELIEF

- The world we live in has been built by those who ignored their critics.

RULE-BREAKING ATTITUDE

• Richard Branson, founder of the Virgin Group, once said, "You don't learn to walk by following rules. You learn by doing, and by falling over."

RESOURCEFULNESS

• Entrepreneurs create a path where before there was none. Combine these traits with a good idea that fills a need and you have a recipe for success. The idea itself and the infrastructure for making it happen can be easily passed down to the next generation, but the personality traits necessary to follow in their parents footsteps and build on that success are the tricky part. You can't change who your children are or determine what they will become, but you can give them every opportunity to discover their own inner entrepreneur. The best teacher is you.

ENCOURAGING THE FAMILYPRENEUR

Ford was able to successfully transition his company to his son, who in turn passed it to his son and so on, but most entrepreneurial endeavors fizzle without the vision and passion of the person with the original dream. In 2012, German researchers at The Institute for the Study of Labor (ISL) found that children are 60% more likely to become an entrepreneur when one of their parents is an entrepreneur.[7]

If the second generation is interested in the business and shares the passion of the parent, half the battle has been won. But how do you fan the entrepreneurial flames of what might not be a child's desire to flourish in the footsteps of his or her parent?

---

7 Why Do Entrepreneurial Parents Have Entrepreneurial Children?, MJ Lindquist, The Institute for the Study of Labor, Bonn, Germany, 2012.

How can you assure your business can survive without you? What can you do to increase the likelihood that the second generation wants to participate in and build on your success? How do you foster what I call familypreneurship?

1. LET THEM FIND THEIR OWN PATH

From their earliest years, children naturally form interests and curiosities that should be nurtured and encouraged. As the ISL study found, many children do gravitate toward the work of their parents. Edward Wimmer, co-founder of Road ID, started the business with his father. "I'm pretty sure 'entrepreneur' was one of the first words I knew how to spell. I simply can't remember not wanting to be an entrepreneur. It was a desire ignited by my father...I wanted to be like him."[8]

Brandon Byrd's business, Goodies Frozen Custard & Treats, is a natural extension of his childhood interests. "For me, entrepreneurship started very young. I used to pick up aluminum cans as a kid for extra money. In junior high school, I started selling gummy worms ten for a dollar, and I would net about $150 weekly."[9]

For some kids, the entrepreneurial drive is there from the beginning. But many children of entrepreneurs will have completely different interests. A florist's daughter may want to become an accountant. A corporate executive's son might be an excellent sculptor. All children should be encouraged to do what they love to do, even if it's not the family business.

---

8 http://www.inc.com/jeff-haden/what-inspired-10-successful-entrepreneurs-to-become-entrepreneurs.html
9 38 Black Entrepreneurs Share Origin Stories, Ronald P. Barba,
  http://tech.co/38-black-entrepreneurs-share-origin-stories-2015-02

In 2012, German researchers at The Institute for the Study of Labor (ISL) found that children are 60% more likely to become an entrepreneur when one of their parents is an entrepreneur.

2. MODEL THE ENTREPRENEURIAL SPIRIT

We know that children learn how to become adults by watching their parents. Role modeling entrepreneurial behavior makes children more likely to become aware of it as a career option, or "shaping the child's values, such as a taste for autonomy."[10]

Eric Ripert, co-owner and chef of New York's famed Le Bernardin restaurant, grew up in an entrepreneurialsupported environment. "From a young age, my mother instilled in me a sense of responsibility and inspired me to lead by example. My mother ran a successful home as well as a successful business in fashion. She owned and managed several boutiques. Her aspirations and ambitions encouraged me, even as a child, not only to achieve my goals, but also to become a leader in what I do."[11]

Starting Dog Quality Enterprises, a business to sell products specifically to improve the lives of older dogs and their owners was a passion for Ann-Marie Fleming—a passion she says comes from her father. "He taught me at a very young age that anything is possible — you just need to work hard and believe in yourself. When things go wrong he taught me to break the problem down into bite size pieces and push ahead... I have been empowered by this belief throughout my entire life, something that fuels menow more than ever."[12]

10 The Institute for the Study of Labor, Bonn, Germany, 2012.
11 http://www.inc.com/jeff-haden/what-inspired-10-successful-entrepreneurs-to-becomeentrepreneurs.html
12 http://www.businessnewsdaily.com/1094-father-knew-best-entrepreneurs-tell-how-dadinspired-them.html

When a child grows up in an environment in which they see, every day, the rewards of owning your own business, working for yourself, making your dream become reality, they absorb the mindset and are more likely to want that for themselves. Your child is more likely to develop the determination and the confidence to make their own dreams happen by witnessing you doing the same.

3. EASE THEM INTO IT

For the child who shows an interest and aptitude for becoming an entrepreneur, gaining experience within the family business is invaluable. Giving your child a sense of the satisfaction of running a business while they spend time with you can light his or her enthusiasm.

Billy Bones, founder of Booking Agent Info, credits his parents' willingness to include him in their work as contributing to his own desire to be independent. "When they came to this country, my dad opened up an accounting office and my mom opened up a beauty salon. At an early age, I witnessed my parents working long hours and putting a lot into their businesses. I was often right there with them as a kid helping them where I could."[13]

Tara Jacobson, 44-year old owner of Marketing Artfully, says she has 32 years of business experience thanks to her days working with her parents.

> "They always had retail stores growing up,
> fun little shops that sold books, gifts
> and Christmas items. I can remember grabbing the cash
> box and running up to the store to wait on customers who
> came to visit. That is where I learned to make change,
> interact with all different types of customers and (it)
> generally sparked my entrepreneurial flame!"[14]

13 38 Black Entrepreneurs Share Origin Stories, Ronald P. Barba
14 http://www.businessnewsdaily.com/1094-father-knew-best-entrepreneurs-tell-how-dad-inspired-them.html

Generally speaking, most kids want to be like their parents. We learn how to become a human being, how to walk and talk, how to play, and work, and interact with others by watching the people we are with every single day of our lives from the moment we arrive here—our parents and family. We learn how to become adults by watching our parents as adults. Boys learn how to become a man by watching their fathers and girls learn what it is to be a woman from their mothers. Likewise, entrepreneurs learn to be entrepreneurs from the entrepreneurs right there at home. They learn from parents who encourage them to be whatever they want to be, provide them opportunities to discover what their best choice in career will be, and then support and guide them in their journey, wherever it may lead them.

ACTIVITY: "MOM, DAD, HOW DID YOU DO IT?"

There is no better resource for your child to discover what makes the entrepreneur tick than you. You have the story, the legacy and the timeline of your own journey archived in your mind and memory. Share this with your children. Have them interview you. Whether for a school project or just a family activity at home, they can mine their own treasure trove of tips for success right under their noses.

QUESTIONS YOU CAN ENCOURAGE YOUR CHILD TO ASK

Below are a variety of questions to start the process of helping your kids get more engaged with your business:

- How did you get your idea or concept for the business?

- What attributes have made you successful?

- What makes your business unique?

- What advice would you give me to make sure I follow in your footsteps?

- If you had the chance to start your career over again, what would you do differently?

- What would you say are the top three skills needed to be a successful entrepreneur?

- What have been some of your failures, and what have you learned from them?

- Describe/outline your typical day?

- How has being an entrepreneur affected your family life?

- What motivates you?

- What would say are the five key skills needed to run a successful business?

For every light bulb, car and iPhone, there are thousands of smaller innovations, inventions, products and ideas that are changing the world in small, but still greatly impactful ways every day. For every Edison, Ford, and Jobs, there are multitudes of shop owners, small businessmen and women, freelancers, and other entrepreneurs filling needs in society and achieving success while supporting a family, making their dreams come true and inspiring others to do the same. You've discovered that joy and with your encouragement, love, guidance, and support, your children can too.

Perhaps the only thing more rewarding than becoming a successful entrepreneur is raising a successful familypreneur at the same time. In the next chapter I'll share more ideas to help you inspire your children through a variety of creative methods, to follow.

CHAPTER THREE

Step two

Tap Into Your Dreams to Build Their Dreams

You've dreamed of having your children involved in your business since the day they were born. You saw, early on, that they had the ability to take over your company one day because you saw they were strong and curious and smart as soon as they started walking and talking.

Now it's been some years and you continue to see potential in them. They may be approaching an age when they are even able to help you by getting involved in some way in your business. What's your next best move to get them interested? You don't wan to be pushy? You are wondering things like, "How do I start the conversation to get them interested in working with me?"

HOW DO YOU FOLLOW THROUGH ON YOUR DREAMS TO BUILD THEIR DREAMS?

There are a number of ways you can start connecting the dream you have to the dreams you wish your children would also adopt. The important thing to do is to, first, go deeper in your own dream. This is about getting more involved in your company outside of the workplace. Following are just a few of the ways you can create this bridge that runs from you to your children:

• *Find non-profits that offer events where you can involve your children.* For example, take the YWCA that provides all kinds of programs that help disadvantaged women get help with their careers and for their children. They have a number of events where you can bring your kids to help women and their families.

• *Take your kids to the library.* Library discussions that might be in some way connected to your business could be great settings to get your kids interested in your business.

• *Buy Entrepreneurial Kits for Kids.* Check out the site Bizz in a Box (http://www.bizinaboxx.com/) It's filled with great kits that get kids involved with entrepreneurship. Starting its offerings from 7 on up, these kits could be just the tools that get your kids engaged in your business.

IDENTIFY YOUR CHILD'S UNIQUE PASSIONS

Your goal here should be to connect your children's passions to those parts of your business that are in some way related. What might this look like? Let's say you own a florist business and your child doesn't have a penchant for design or anything related to plants and flowers.

But let's further say your child is a creative. She likes to paint and creates unique birthday cards where she writes poems to her relatives for their special days. You might start develop a connection to your business by asking her to write a poem for an upcoming Thanksgiving special you want to advertise on social media. You tell her you will actually pay her for the poem. Now, you have connected to something that she already likes to do and you have also taken her skills and exposure to your business to a new level.

You praise her for her clever poem and also put up the ad on a special poster board that your customers can see when they walk into your store. You point the poster out to them and share that your ten-year old daughter wrote the poem. Of course people will be impressed and the ones who are really excited about your child's poem, well, why not ask if you can take a picture of them holding up the poem giving a "thumbs up" to it. Now, you can take several of those pictures (with your customer's permission, of course) and put them out on Facebook. Now, there is even more spotlighting of your daughter's talents and she feels very included in your business.

Now you have successfully connected a passion she has and have nurtured it. Of course, the next holiday you can ask her if she would like to participate. You downplay her potential participation so that she doesn't feel pressured to participate, but, very likely she will take that opportunity as you tell her something like, "You know Suzie, you really helped me out the last time with my advertising. If you have time and would like to help again, of course I'll pay you. Just let me know if you are interested."

Why downplay her participation? You don't want your child to feel like helping in the business is a chore. Sometimes parents are demanding of the children involving themselves in their parents' business. This sets up a resistance as they feel an obligation rather than seeing the participation as an opportunity. You don't want your good intentions to turn on you. So, instead, you are subtle. You take your time to nurture the interest that you have ignited.

Finally, it's not about trying just one or two things, but a number of things. Also, what may work for one of your children might now work for another. So experiment. There are so many options today and surely more will be emerging over time. Just be patient and keep looking for ways to make your dreams relevant to their lives and you will find yourself on the right path. That's just what I will show you how to do in the next chapter.

CHAPTER FOUR

Step three

Prepare Your Young FamilyPreneur

Not long ago, it was common, even expected, that a newly-degreed college graduate would apply, interview for, and accept an entrylevel job at an established company, learn the business and slowly rise through the hierarchy based on merit and seniority. These companies offered employment benefits, and a "job for life"—a steady income into retirement and an early retirement as a result of solid, robust pension plan. Job security and perks were the backbone of corporate careers for decades.

I believe the job for life is still achievable in small family businesses. When children are introduced to the concept at a young age an integrated into a shared, familypreneur mindset, they are more likely to choose to contribute, participate and eventually work in all aspects of the family business. The corporate career is no longer the safe bet it once was. There is no company loyalty anymore, as restructuring, mergers, acquisitions, spinoffs, layoffs, and downsizing are all too often the reality. Joining your small business venture can provide your child with a more stable and secure career. At the same time, it helps ensure the continuity of your business and lays the groundwork for long-term succession planning.

Although you must allow your children to choose their own career paths, you do have the ability to help them build the skills necessary to become a successful entrepreneur. I can't emphasize enough that the earlier you engage your kids in all aspects of the family business, the more appealing and attractive that life may appear to them down the road. Take the Reddick family, for example.

The Reddick family owns and runs a small paper products company. Dick and Nancy Reddick always intended for their children to become involved in the business and eventually take over. When they were young, the children worked in the warehouse at their own choosing. "The children had to decide for themselves that they wanted to be a part of it," Nancy says. "In our early years, we made some bad business choices, but one thing we did right was giving the kids the choice to do whatever they wanted with their lives. We didn't force them into the business. There were no expectations."

The Reddicks made sure their children got out into the world before settling on a career at their paper company. The Reddick children made life choices that spread them out across the country, eventually leading back home to work with their parents, just as Dick and Nancy hoped. But when the children returned as adults, they brought with them a unique set of experiences to draw from, which inspired fresh thinking and bold new ideas that reenergized the business.

The Reddicks also allowed their children to determine which business discipline was their calling. "They needed to figure out for themselves what roles within the business they were best suited for. We couldn't do that for them," said Nancy.

Their daughter Luisa says her parents allowed the children to make their own mistakes. "While I still rely on my father for so many things, like his strong palate, one of the keys to the success of our business has been that our father was willing to step aside," she said. "He let me make the same mistakes he did. He never said, 'Well, I've done that, and it doesn't work.'"

The Reddicks are a great example of the benefits of family dynamics in the entrepreneurial setting. Their paper products company has provided a unifying mission that brings them together and strengthens—not strains—the familial bonds. They share in a mission that benefits them all.

FINDING THEIR NICHE

While young children are often enthusiastic about helping at the family store, restaurant or business, as they grow, their interests and desires may change. Their enthusiasm may wane, much to the chagrin of their parents. But your child's interest and involvement is a bonus rather than a guarantee of lifelong participation. It is part of their journey and encouraging them along the way is critical.

Of course there are great benefits to having your children employed by the family company. Aside from clear tax advantages, your child can use the business to experiment and explore the various business disciplines to discover where their genuine interests lie. One child may be drawn to sales and marketing, while another develops a desire to solve customer problems. Whichever area appeals to them, it is up to you as a parent to nurture their knowledge and confidence, and guide the development of basic skills that will increase their likelihood of success no matter what they choose to do. Allowing your children a window on the business world, teaching them how and why you do what you love, the more likely they are to want to find the door.

Let's say you run a small cupcake business. On the surface, any child would have some natural curiosity about a store that sells delicious sweet treats, but as a child of the proprietor, they get the experience of learning the day-to-day operation and what it takes to make the best cupcakes and get them to the most people while realizing the highest possible profit. They will learn the subtle and not-so-subtle importance of location, advertising, product differentiation, supply and demand, and direct market competition. The more they know about the trials and triumphs of making and selling cupcakes, the more they can make an informed decision about joining you in the venture.

As your children mature, you can encourage their interests and develop their inherent talents by finding creative ways to integrate them into your business. Lisa may be a financial genius but a disaster in the kitchen. Ask him to help handle the books rather than bake cakes. Jamal might be shy and cerebral and more suited to working behind the scenes rather than talking to customers at the register. By giving your children tasks that showcase their strengths, they are more likely to stay interested in the business and flourish in the long term.

Like anything else, it starts with education. Providing your child with the best possible education, whatever form it may take, is the greatest gift we can give them. The goal within your household should be constant learning and personal development; taking courses, upgrading skills, pursuing new interests, reading, watching or listening to contemporary thinkers. You can't assume your child will pursue an MBA in order to take over the family business. That kinesiology degree may not seem useful to the family cupcake business, but the overall skills your child will acquire by dedicating themselves to the completion of that accomplishment will provide vital skills that will benefit them in invaluable ways.

Let them play, experiment, and grow. When they get old enough, let them take on other responsibilities within the company. You may be surprised and find that the child you thought had no interest in taking over the family business finds their niche—the result of a seed that was planted many years earlier.

To help your child find what they love, there are five important factors to consider.

1. THERE IS NO SUCH THING AS STARTING TOO YOUNG

Legendary investor and billionaire Warren Buffet claims to have purchased his first stock at the age of twelve. He also says he started too late. If you are a first generation entrepreneur, you started because the passion burned inside you and could not be ignored. You sleep, eat and dream your business, days, nights, and weekends. We've already seen in earlier examples that stoking that fire in your children and providing the learning environment that serves as an incubator for creativity, exploration and discovery is critical from their earliest days.

2. THE BENEFITS OF RESPONSIBILITY

There is something noble about stepping up to a challenge, taking a risk, and putting everything you have into making a familyoperated business a success. There is courage and strength in accepting a failure and pushing through to a greater success. So whether it is a lemonade stand, an art sale, a plant sale at school, or offering to pull the neighbor's weeds, encourage your children to do it themselves. Provide the tools they need, set them up for success and let them go. Grow their responsibilities as their capabilities and experience grow. Involve your children in decisions and encourage them to contribute ideas. You may not want to implement everything they suggest, but discuss with them how their ideas can be shaped to become feasible. Some ideas will miss the mark, others may be interesting, and some may be valuable. Give your children an opportunity to see their ideas become reality and give them some responsibility to make them succeed.

If you own a plant and flower nursery and your young son has an idea to have a flower sale for Mother's Day, let him be responsible for watering them, protecting them from pests, and harvesting them when the time is right. Perhaps your daughter doesn't like to get her hands dirty, she could assemble boxes and select the plants for shipping. Allowing them to have small responsibilities at an early age will give them a sense of purpose and value. Rewarding them for their creativity and contributions instills that pride of accomplishment so crucial in building self-esteem and confidence.

3. FAILURE IS AS VALUABLE AS SUCCESS

We must also let our children fail. This is a very important point. Allow them to make mistakes and hold them accountable as you would any other employee. I have a friend who teaches at an urban high school. He often comments that parents are far more interested in making things easy for their children rather than allowing them to experience the consequences of their actions. "Helicopter parenting" has become too common in our homes and millennials, through no fault of their own, are widely seen to be entitled and averse to failing.

In the flower nursery example, inventory must be watered regularly or it dies. If your daughter is responsible for watering the plants and she doesn't, there are consequences for the business. When your son does a good job de-budding the mums, he sees the positive result in the beautiful flowers he has helped create. If you want success for your children, teach them that what they do matters.

4. TAKING PRIDE IN THE WORK

I have close friends who run a business and make a point to "leave work at work." For some, separating work from their personal or home life is necessary and a sign that perhaps that passion for what they do has faded over time and become more stressful than enjoyable. Your children will learn from this too. When we don't talk about our work at home, we not only deprive our children the opportunity to learn about what we do, but we also send vague signals that we may not enjoy it and would rather avoid thinking about it. Our personal emotions and view can directly influence and color your child's attitudes about your company, your job, and the satisfaction you may or may not derive from it. You don't want your kids to grow up thinking the family business was a walk in the park, but you don't want them to think it was a negative experience either. Challenging times or even the failure of a family business can be tremendous opportunities to educate our children about the risk of doing business. We can model dignity and strength in the face of disappointment, and turn it into a deeper determination and drive to try again.

5. THE WORLD OUTSIDE YOUR WALLS

Encourage your children to work outside your family company for a period of time, even if their goal is take over your business one day. Doing so will help them develop an appreciation for your business and allow them to experience different management styles. You can sweeten the deal by offering them a higher-level position or a bonus when they return to your company, but any time spent working in other industries and for other companies will pay dividends to your child and to your business.

TEACHING BASIC SKILLS

By raising our children in an environment that encourages creativity and exploration, we are providing them with the best possible start to becoming who they want to be. With that, they need some basic knowledge, skills and tools that are common to all successful entrepreneurs.

An elementary school near my home in Alberta, Canada implemented a leadership program initiative in the last few years. Titled "The Leader In Me," the initiative was inspired by Dr. Stephen R. Covey's best-selling book The 7 Habits of Highly Effective People.[15] It teaches children practical life and leadership skills and encourages a culture in which every child has an opportunity to become a leader.

In the years since implementing the program, school administrators have seen tremendous changes in many of the students' outlook and approach to various life situations. An important element of the program is to encourage conversation and learning at home—a fantastic opportunity for parents. This program and others like it are doing great things in our schools but they are a single drop in a very big ocean. We can't rely on schools alone to give our children what they need. Schools, even the best ones, can only do so much with shrinking funding and resources and the limited time they have with your children. Teaching our children and equipping them with the necessary skills to become successful in life and in business starts in your home. If you view your child's education as a responsibility that begins with you, he or she is far more likely to have what it takes to succeed.

15 Visit http://www.theleaderinme.org

Beyond, reading, writing, math, science and the other basic subjects taught at school, the foundation of every successful entrepreneur can be attributed to four basic skills; communication, time management, financial literacy, and self-discipline. The importance of these for anyone is well documented and they are skills many adults don't adequately develop. They are often overlooked at school, especially in the earlier grades, and we are left to the trial and error of daily life to learn these things, sometimes with painful lessons.

But, as parents, there are many things we can do at home to teach these things to our children, at almost any age. Here are some activities I recommend to help you. You can adapt any of these for younger children as well as those of high school age.

EDUCATIONAL ACTIVITIES TO TRY AT HOME

Following are a series of things you can choose to do with your children on a regular basis, right in the comfort of your home. Try to turn these activities into part of the fabric of your daily lives so that your children come to not only expect them, but to also look forward to them.

EFFECTIVE COMMUNICATION

To effectively communicate, children need to be able to say what they mean to help others understand what they want. Giving directions is a great way to practice this skill.

Think of a local landmark in your town or neighborhood that you and your child are familiar with. Ask your child to write down directions for how to get there from your home. (No cell phones! This is one for pen and paper. No mobile devices allowed.)

Take a little trip with your child, following the directions exactly as she wrote them. Discuss them along the way. Are they easy to follow? Did you get lost or did they help you find where you were going? How could they have been better? Could they be clearer?

THE MOMENT BEFORE AND AFTER

The ability to understand the logical progression of events provides context to everything that happens around us. We need to understand cause and effect. Find a picture of people performing a task; firemen putting out a fire, a plumber fixing a drain, a person waiting for a bus. Ask your child what might have happened just before the picture was taken. What were the people in the picture doing an hour before? What will they do an hour after? Make a game of it. It can be fun to observe people in public places and devise stories of the moments before and after.

THE EXPERT SPEECH

Being able to speak intelligently about a topic is critical in all walks of life. To practice, have your child choose any topic that interests them, and ask them to stand up in the middle of a room and tell you and other family members about that topic for two minutes without stopping. Adjust the number of minutes and the topics depending on the child's age. Try assigning them topics on which they need to justify an opinion or topics with which they aren't very familiar and need to improvise.

SOMEONE ELSE'S SHOES

Empathy and the ability to understand someone else's situation are critical to being an effective leader. Ask your children to name an occupation. They might say teacher or police officer. Next, ask them to name three emotions. They'll answer with happiness, sadness, fear, etc. Now ask them to pretend they are that person feeling each of those emotions. They would act out a teacher being happy, and then, sad, and then fearful. Then, do the same thing as a police officer. Discuss the differences. What made each of them unique? How do we know it is a teacher who is sad versus a police officer? Why do they feel that way?

PASS THE BUCK

This is a great activity to teach listening skills. During a discussion with more than two people, anytime someone talks, they hold a dollar bill. No one else is allowed to speak without having that dollar bill in his or her hand. When the person with the dollar is done talking, they pass it to the person who wants to respond or talk next. Try this at the dinner table or when the family is together. Ask everyone to talk about their day, best friend, favorite movie, or any other topic everyone will be able to respond to. Only the person with the dollar can speak. Everyone else should be listening.

TIME MANAGEMENT

SIMPLE WEEKLY CHECKLIST

This is a common activity in many homes and an effective tool for helping your child adhere to deadlines and manage the things they need to do in the time they have. Help your child draw a chart or design one on the computer or tablet. Along the top, have him write the days of the week. Down the left side, list the jobs, chores, or homework that needs to be done after school each day. Have them check off the boxes each day when they complete a task. Each evening or at the end of the week, have a conversation about what was or wasn't done and how time could have been managed or tasks adjusted to get everything done.

WHAT IS MOST IMPORTANT?

Sometimes there isn't enough time to do everything we want to do and we have to make choices. Prioritizing is a skill even many adults have trouble with. Have your child make a list of the top five most important things in their life in any given week. Have a discussion about what's most important and least important. Rank them. For example, the list might look like this:

1. School and homework
2. Soccer practice
3. My dog
4. Playing with friends
5. Watching TV

Talk about what would happen if they were invited to a friend's birthday party but had homework that night; or they wanted to play with the dog after school but had soccer practice; or their favorite television show was on and the dog needed to be fed. Discuss how decisions about how they use their time depend on what their priorities are. If we have our priorities set, decisions become easier to make.

FINANCIAL LITERACY

CREDITS FOR CASH

There are many ways to teach your child the value of finishing what they started, earning money, and working for what they want. Giving an allowance is an option, but it's much better to have them earn it. Set up a simple system by which your child earns a number of credits for finishing activities, jobs around the house, homework, etc. Set a value for each activity. Set a rule that at the end of the week, the allowance will only be given if a certain number of points have been accumulated that week. Award points for good behavior or going above and beyond expectations. Subtract points as punishment for poor behavior.

Each week, discuss how the point total was or wasn't reached and what could've been done differently.

YOUR CHILD'S OWN BUDGET

Budgeting is another skill that is universally valuable and it's never too early to learn how to do it and stick to it. Using pen and paper or any number of apps or online tools, you can help children of almost any age design a budget that is as simple or complex as necessary. Discuss with your child their income (everything from allowance, gifts or babysitting money to a part-time job), and their expenses (food, movies, video games, music, gas, car payment, clothing, etc.). Talk about known expenses and unknown expenses, things that may come up that we are unable to anticipate. Help your child make a budget for an entire month. Discuss where the money is going, what they can or can't afford, how they may need to save to be able to afford something they want.

SELF-DISCIPLINE

STICK TO A ROUTINE

Children thrive under rules and routine. Even having a set number of activities that are done every day at the same time provides structure and accountability. Brushing their teeth, making their bed, cleaning their room, feeding the dog, and other household habits are valuable ways to learn self-discipline.

SPORTS, THE ARTS AND OTHER ACTIVITIES

Being involved in any sport, playing an instrument, joining a club or church group are all activities that require commitment. Learning to fulfill their commitments, even when they don't feel like it or would rather do something else, is a lesson all children need to learn. Teams and groups rely on the contribution of each member and provide a sense of shared accomplishment.

MODELING SELF-DISCIPLINE

One of the best things you can do for your child is to teach by example. We've discussed the importance of modeling the behaviors, skills and attitudes we want our child to have and showing self-discipline is no different. You know this already if you've ever tried to get your child to make their bed everyday when they know you don't. If we live our lives taking shortcuts and letting things slide, our children will too.

There are hundreds of resources available to help you teach these things to your child and I urge you to seek them out and use what's best for you and your family. But whatever you choose, these four skills are critical, whatever career or vocation your child chooses. Praise and positive reinforcement are essential. Rewards for good behavior and consequences for bad are unquestionably beneficial. Rules and structure are necessary. Whether you're raising an entrepreneur or not, your child needs to know how to communicate and listen, win and lose, succeed and fail, show up on time, get things done, earn, spend and save money, play and work well with others, and love what they do and who they are.

CHAPTER FIVE

Step four

Involve Your Child in Your Business to
Gain the FamilyPreneur Perspective

One evening as my family sat around the dinner table, I asked my six and seven-year old sons if they knew what I did every day when I went to work. They were a bit surprised by the question and avoided answering it. But, I insisted. My youngest was the first to raise his hand. "Dad, I know what you do," he said. "You just go and sit in front of a computer and you punch on it the whole day. Then, you come back home later in the evening." I turned to my oldest son whose blank expression told me he had no clue whatsoever of what I did for a living.

Two days later, while driving my three-year-old daughter home from the daycare, she asked me to buy her some candy; I told her that I had no money that day. She made it quite clear that she was disappointed, not to mention a little incredulous. "Dad, you have money," she insisted, "I saw you drive to that building and put a card in the machine, and the money came out! Why can't you do it now?"

Over the next couple of days, I thought a lot about these conversations and wondered why my kids, especially the oldest, had no idea how I make a living and no idea, either, about how we have the life we enjoy, with a comfortable home, a car, plenty of food and clothes. That's when it occurred to me that it was time to begin teaching my children some important lessons to help them make the connection between the comforts they enjoy with the work required to provide them.

You might wonder if it's too soon to start teaching children — at three, six and seven years of age – about the economic realities of adult life. Now is the perfect time to start, especially if you own your own business.

Many successful small business owners end up closing their doors or selling their business to a third party because their grown children and other family members have no interest in taking over the business when they retire. This sad statistic illustrates that today's business owners are missing an opportunity to teach their kids about the business and the many benefits that owning a small business can provide. The earlier you start to teach your children, the better the chances are that they will want to follow in your footsteps and lead the business you built for them into the future.
This cannot be forced. Like all parents, you want your children to be happy, which means allowing them the space to choose their own career path. It is mportant to understand, too, that one or more of your children may not be suited for running a business.

In this chapter, I'll provide some ideas that will help your children learn to look at your business as an integral part of your family's lifestyle, making the connections between your family business and the life they enjoy.

1. MARKET THE FAMILY BUSINESS TO YOUR KIDS

It is said that the most important marketing job family business owners have is that of selling the business to their children as both a career and strengthening the family unit. This exchange must begin as soon as the children are capable of understanding. Understand that your business might not be suited for some or all of your offspring. You must give them room to choose their own career paths, but you can improve the way they view and appreciate your business.

"Dad, I know what you do.
You type on a computer all day!"

Tell them the story of how you (or your predecessors) started the business. This is something you can do at an early age. Be careful not to overly dramatize the saga, but help them to understand why you (and your spouse, because he/she is involved whether they actively work in the business or not) started the enterprise.

2. SHOW THEM HOW YOU DO BUSINESS

Take them to work with you. Many second generation business owners express fond memories of going to work with their parents in the business on Saturday mornings. They had the opportunity to get to know the employees and customers and got to see first-hand how their parents operated their business. For many, their love and devotion to the family business – and the pride of ownership – began with those early visits.

3. MAKE TIME TO EXPLAIN TO THEM WHAT YOU DO

Tell your kids about why you're in business. Let them know who your customers are and how your products or services help make their lives better. Your customers purchase from your business for a reason, and how they use your products or services. Without boasting, let them know you are proud of the business in which you are engaged and how it benefits others. Tell them success stories.

4. MAKE THEM FEEL INVESTED IN YOUR BUSINESS

As your children grow, give them the opportunity to work in the business. Working in the family business can become a source of pride for your children if presented as an opportunity rather than a requirement. Many parents worry that children don't learn responsibility soon enough and insist that they go to work in the company so they can teach them the value of hard work and how to earn money. There's nothing wrong with giving them chores to do around the house or even insisting that they get part-time jobs, but do not force them to come to work in your business. Give them the opportunity and make it attractive enough that they will enjoy the work. A 10 year-old might enjoy helping stuff envelopes for a mailing, counting inventory or other age-appropriate activity. But, do not give them the jobs nobody else wants, like emptying the trash. Earning a few dollars and enjoying the experience can go a long way toward forming a positive attitude about your business. When compensating them, always pay what the job is worth. Don't underpay because you can get away with it or overpay because they are family. The sooner it is understood that compensation is based on the value of a job, the better everyone will be. There is also an added benefit in paying your kids for the work they do. It gives them an income that they must learn to manage, which leads into my next recommendation

5. TEACH THEM THE VALUE OF MONEY

I have always been a keen observer of parents and kids in a grocery; the younger ones to a certain extent would like to buy whatever they want; it doesn't matter if you talked about the behaviour before you entered the store – just keep your hands to yourself!

Visits to the store offer tremendous, teachable moments—opportunities to help your children learn more about business. For example, you can ask them about the different products they see and how useful they are. Ask them if they know how those products got there on the shelf. You can use price as the context for all sorts of questions about how much it might have cost to make the product, if the price would cover the costs and how much profit the manufacturer might make as well as the store that sells it. Equally, you can help them transfer these ideas and concepts to the family business environment. Just as in a grocery store, your family business is not an island – it operates because it transacts with other businesses and individuals.

DO THESE IDEAS REALLY WORK?

After employing all of these ideas with my own children, two years after that initial dinner table conversation with my sons, I asked them again if they knew what I did for a living. Their answers were astonishing. This time, it was my younger son who was the first to raise his hand. He said, "Dad, I have been observing what you do. I even visited your work website. I heard you saying at the dinner table that you had to work on a Saturday because of a busy season. One of your duties is to help people with their personal taxes."

The answer was impressive! Then, I went on and asked: "What do you know about taxes?" He said, "People and businesses pay taxes to the government and the government uses the money to build roads and schools." The conversation was getting interesting. Before I could even ask he said: "I heard about taxes on TV." Not only was he learning about my business, he was also making connections between our conversations and what he was seeing on TV! Then my older son chimed in, saying, "I saw you reading tables and graphs and you had made notes like the company was making losses." In just two years, my sons had not only a better understanding of the work I do, but a real interest in it. With some additional information from me to round out the story, moving forward I had no doubt that the kids could understand what I did for a living.

WOULD YOU END UP DOING THE SAME THING AS MOM AND DAD?

Many parents have tried to talk their kids into joining the family business and eventually take it over, but were told NO! I have always wondered why the majority of kids refuse to join and learn their parent's business. Is it because they feel like the parents are imposing on them their will? Is it because they don't understand what they do? Are the kids not informed enough about the ins and outs of running a business? Are they simply scared of the dedication and requirements to operate a small business? Do they not see the incentive to work hard given the parents have already paved the way for a seemingly comfortable future?

I would say, the biggest issue is, lack of knowledge and understanding of the business itself. Sheltering or waiting for your children to be of the 'right' age to introduce them to what it takes to operate your small business, is too late. They have already made up their minds at this point.

A FAMILYPRENEUR PERSPECTIVE BUILDS ON A CONTINUUM OF LEARNING

Consider the process of teaching your kids discipline, etiquette and manners. It doesn't start when your child is fifteen when they are about to start high school. You should teach all of the above when they are very young so that they grow up knowing what makes up socially acceptable behaviors.

Equally, it's the same thing with business. If you teach your kids at an early age, they will develop their own understanding based on what you have taught them. The chances are greater that they will end up coming and working with you. In other words, you have given them the opportunity to move through the following stages, (complements of Melissa G Wilson, a marketing expert):

> *Awareness.* They were presented with the idea of entrepreneurship at a very young age when they didn't have any negative filters built up from the outside world. They just had your enthusiasm and passion that you showed them.

Recognition. You created that bridge or those bridges between your business and the dreams you have about it and their dreams for their futures. Again, you started building these bridges when they were very young and now their connection to you and your business is part of the fabric of their lives.

Ownership. They're in. They can't see their lives evolve in any other way but as stewards of your business. They are those special people who will be given the opportunity to carry on the good work you started. This knowledge gives them great satisfaction, reducing the real worry that so many young people experience, first, going off to college, trying to figure out what they will do with their lives, and, then, after college, again, trying to figure out what will be their destiny.

Leverage. You have not only created a successful entrepreneurial succession plan for your children, but, also, for their children. It's all because of the infrastructure and solid set of practices you created to nurture them into success.

You have helped your children form positive attitudes and feelings around what what you do. Thus, if you ask them what they would like to do with their live., the family business will most likely be part of the conversation.

Take the example of top athletes. There are lots of success stories where kids followed their parents' footsteps and became athletes themselves. Why? Because they were immersed in the culture of the sport and also the day-to-day experiences surrounding the job. And in most cases, these experiences were positive motivators to do the same thing when they grew up. The same process works regarding family businesses. You have built it and they have connected.

A FAMILYPRENEUR PERSPECTIVE BUILDS
ON A CONTINUUM OF LEARNING

Imagine if you didn't start teaching your children discipline, etiquette and manners until they started high school at age fifteen. You would have had a pretty rough time with them at home but they also would have struggled out in the world interacting with others. Instinctively, we know that we need to start teaching these things as early as possible, perhaps even before they understand.

Teaching business is no different. By educating your children at an early age about what you do, they will develop their own understanding based on what you teach and show them. The chances are greater that they will develop an interest in business in general, if not your business, because they grew up with it. They have formed a positive attitude and will associate good feelings around what their parents do. Ideally, as they mature and you begin to discuss with them their own aspirations and dreams of a career, the family business will become part of the conversation.

Not long ago, a friend of mine took his sons to see their first major league baseball game. The Texas Rangers were in town and the first baseman that day was Prince Fielder. He recalled watching his father Cecil Fielder hit home runs for the Detroit Tigers back in the 1990s. Though the memory made me feel old, it was yet another teachable moment.

As a young boy, Prince Fielder spent summers in the team's dugout and the clubhouse with his father in those early years. Being around baseball created memories associated with the game and, along with his close relationship with his father, inspired him to pursue professional baseball himself.

Children whose parents ran a small business, like those I mentioned in Chapter 2, have similar stories to tell. Positive associations, happy memories and feeling a sense of belonging and importance are powerful influencers in a young child's development. Your business (yes, even a personal tax business) can and should be as much a part of your children's lives as it is yours.

CHAPTER SIX

Step five

Build Your Child's Business Knowledge

You may be asking about now, what do you do once your children do take an interest in your business and now want to be a part of your company's future? Now it's time to go the next level. This is about teaching your children the foundational elements of a successful business.

Your child may already be familiar with basic terminology from exposure to media. We are bombarded daily with the stock market index, oil prices, interest rates, and exchange rates. While it is valuable information and worth knowing, I have always wondered why we hear very little information in the mainstream media relevant to the small business owner. Small businesses are an integral part of the world economy. I believe more media attention should be focused on aspects of our economy important to small businesses, such as housing starts, retail sales reports, and the small business index. Giving these greater visibility would increase awareness of such an important economic demographic, while educating our young people about the benefits and challenges of being a small business owner.

I've shared resources in earlier chapters for your child to have a more hands-on experience. There are also dozens of excellent websites, programs and even summer camps available to teach business skills to your children. But I also believe the best education can come from you and your own business.

TEACHING BUSINESS CONCEPTS

I sometimes take my young sons for a drive to the downtown area of the city where we live. We usually stop for treats and one day, I decided to challenge the boys. We were browsing at Walmart and inevitably found ourselves in the candy aisle. As usual, they were overwhelmed with their choices and stood staring at shelves and shelves of sweets any dentist would sternly advise against.

As they pondered such a critical decision in their young lives, I asked them to stop and take a moment to think about some questions I posed:
- How were these candies made?
- Who made them?
- How did they get to the store and on the shelves?
- Why does Walmart sell the candies?
- Why would people buy candy here instead of going to a candy store?

Predictably they looked at me like I was nuts and they didn't have much to say. This was not, I decided, a teachable moment.

But it occurred to me how valuable it would be for small business owners to teach their children how to analyze the simple business transactions around them. Over time, the children would develop a broad understanding of the systems and processes on which all business is based. The more they know, the more interested they might become.

While a true depth of knowledge of business requires extended training, there are a few foundational concepts that are relevant to any enterprise regardless of size and complexity. The concepts of profit and loss, income and expenses for example are very basic, but key to understanding the management of a business. From there, there are more advanced concepts like supply and demand, inventory control, operations, marketing, sales, production, finance and accounting and so on.

All of these disciplines are addressed in major corporations with layers and layers of employees and executives. Many have gone to school for years to obtain an MBA education in order to advance their careers. However, each of these areas is also necessary in small business but on a much reduced scale. Understanding their application in a small family-owned enterprise doesn't take an MBA, but it does take an understanding of each of these areas.

I have developed an approach that makes it easy to understand the application of the complex mechanics of business to small and medium sized enterprises or SMEs. By bringing these complex ideas down to a smaller scale we can easily see the Core Dynamics of SMEs.

INTRODUCING THE CORE DYNAMICS OF SMALL AND MEDIUM ENTERPRISES

Small and medium-sized businesses are at a great disadvantage when it comes to resources required to drive their organization forward. SME's can't afford the luxury of hiring separate managers to oversee finance, operations, technology, marketing, strategy and planning. But SME's need these skills and resources to fully unlock their potential. Clearly, all businesses need to spend money to make money, but how can the small entrepreneur address these critical areas, adopt best practices and drive the business to optimum growth?

Ideally, small business owners would integrate the Core Dynamics into the regular management discussion and ensure that employees appreciate, analyze and value these dynamics as a unified program driving the business forward.

Owners and senior staff should constantly analyze theirbusiness through the lens of these Core Dynamics. The resulting perspective will lead the management team into a detailed approach to identifying, documenting and designing plans to solve important issues that need attention.

There are four core areas critical to the management of every business:

- Financial Performance

- Management and Operations

- Resources and Processes

- Planning

These four areas work as a unit and should be applied constantly by management to analyze overall performance.

Small and Medium Enterprise Core Dynamics

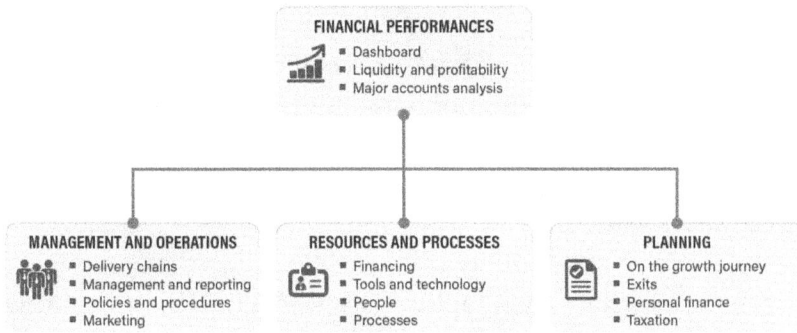

Let's take a look at each of the four core areas.

FINANCIAL PERFORMANCE

Financial performance—the bottom line—is usually captured by a typical business dashboard using data extracted from quarterly bookkeeping records. The information on the dashboard generates multiple questions about the business that need to be answered routinely—questions like the following:

- What is pushing our revenues into growth mode?

- Have we increased the price?

- Is it because of volume increase?

- Why are costs taking a nosedive?

- What are our cost structures?

- Are there costs not recorded in the books?

- Can we find a more inexpensive source for raw materials?

While management reviews the indicators to determine profitability and liquidity, the answers come from the other three Core areas, as they are dependent and interconnected.

MANAGEMENT AND OPERATIONS

The effectiveness with which small business are run on a daily basis directly affects financial performance. "If we improved our operations and changed the way we manage staff, would the improvement lead to better financial performance?"

RESOURCES AND PROCESSES

The management of Inventory, supplies, and production is interconnected with the performance of operation and management, and both in turn, move the financial performance needle. "Do we have what we need and are we efficient enough to trigger a continuous growth mode?"

PLANNING

Planning is a continuous process that pushes the other three Core areas forward, keeping the cycle moving. Business owners must have a sound plan to address the other three areas by week, by month, by quarter, by year. "What do we need to do to get to where we want to be?"

The Core Dynamics, when consistently applied, lead management to focus on short-term planning that leads to a long-term plan, addressing everything from growth strategy to risk to tax implications. We can see this clearly by using a checklist.

PLANNING WITH THE SMALL BUSINESS CHECKLIST MATRIX

Many small business owners will tell you they hardly have time to stop and smell the roses, let alone plan. They often don't have a solid plan in place to carefully analyze their business, think strategically and address the business issues affecting their growth. They are reduced to managing the business by cash balance and taxation. "What did I bring in and what do I owe?" If there is enough cash to pay the bills and taxes when due, they are happy.

But you need to manage your business more thoroughly to unlock its full potential. By using the Small Business Checklist Matrix, you can easily see the application of otherwise complex business management concepts to your small business. Just as the manufacturer of your car advises you to perform regular maintenance and your dentist wants you to have scheduled check ups, your business needs the same attention.

Many small business owners feel their annual tax season trip to the accountant constitutes their yearly "check-up." They leave themselves vulnerable the rest of the year and may be in for a major surprise they could have foreseen had they paid closer attention all year long.

Quarterly reviews would certainly improve the successful longevity of your business. That is why I recommend using the Small Business Checklist Matrix.

The matrix is designed so that key business health checks are identified and addressed using a simple grading system of priority – low, medium and high. The matrix will not only help you track your current situation, but highlight key actions that need to be taken to achieve a specific goal – cost control, adequate financing, financial performance, and planning.

SBC Matrix

	PRIORITY			
	LOW	MED	HIGH	
A. FINANCIAL PERFORMANCES				Cash flows and liquidity
				Profitability (sales, gross margin, incomes, expenses and profits)
				Return on investment and asset utilization
B. MANAGEMENT & OPERATIONS				Location, distribution channels and marketing.
				Management reporting, internal controls, policies and procedures
				Key business processes
C. FINANCING, INVESTING & RESOURCES				Financing or funding effectiveness
				Technologies, tools and equipment
				Staff resources (skill set and compensation strategies)
D. PLANNING (MEDIUM TO LONG TERM)				Business planning and strategies (start up, growth, expansion, maturity, windup)
				Risks Assessment (insurance, economic, social and technological)
				Personal financial planning (retirement, succession and estate)

TO DO:

The Small Business Checklist Matrix should be incorporated into the quarterly business discussions where performances are reviewed.

Your children can role play here, participating first as observers, eventually develop overall business knowledge, enabling them to see the business as a series of interdependent disciplines working together, instead of a tangle of disconnected functions. They will begin to see how things work and how each Core area affects the others.

The matrix may also draw the family's attention to other critical decisions such as personal financial planning and insurance— not as isolated decisions, but as integral parts of managing the business.

THE ROLLING BALL EFFECT

Managing a business is a journey. Using the Core Dynamics and the matrix will help embed a structural approach to reviewing performances. It will also set the foundation of your business in sound fundamentals, which could be transferred to the next generation.

You're no doubt familiar with the idea of viewing your business from 30,000 feet to get a sense of the big picture. From that vantage point, I see every business as a ball slowly rolling down a hill, taking with it all the challenges and problems it faces. But these business realities, if addressed in the right way, step by step, will spur an owner on a growth journey beyond his or her imagination. In the end, the ball will be pushed back up the hill, step by step, to a successful conclusion.

BRINGING IT ALL TOGETHER

In the previous chapters, I laid out several areas where you can educate your children and provide them with the tools and skills they'll need to follow your lead. They may not excel in every area, and they may not show interest at first. Be patient. Bring them along at their own pace taking into consideration what they want and what they are drawn to.

All of the things I've laid out—foundational skills, basic business concepts, and the Core Dynamics can be summed up in a simple, four-step process I'll refer to using the acronym: DUEA. You can use this as a template and philosophy for training your children to become familypreneurs. The acronym represents four simple words that are the true essence of what we need to teach our children:

- Discovery

- Understanding

- Education

- Action

DISCOVERY

Take your children to work with you from an early age. In many instances, the love and passion for the family business will start with those early visits. Include your children in the work of thebusiness. Engage them. Give them a job or a duty where they can learn and understand the benefits of their accomplishments. Add a financial incentive, if possible. The goal here is for your children to learn the value and rewards of hard work.

UNDERSTAND

The main goal you should have for your kids is to have them understand what you do each day for work. Just like them, you wake up in the morning, get dressed and go off into the world. But when you are out of their sight, what is it that you want them to understand you do? For young children, your day can be explained quite simply, without a lot of detail:

- How do you get to work?

- What part of the city do you work in?

- What do you do when you get there?

- What do you eat?

- Who do you talk to daily?

- How many people work with you?

- Do you sell things?

- Do you make things?

- What time do you finish?

For older kids and teens, you can go into more detail. Explain and show the correlation between the life they are living and the family business that has made that lifestyle possible. Share with them questions they could be asking you, such as:

- Why do you go in to work so early?

- Why do you wear a coat and tie?

- How do you decide whom to hire?

- What do you look for in a quality worker?

- What are your tasks?

- What is your management style?

- What is your vision for your business?

- Are you achieving your vision?

- What happens if you don't?

The more information you can offer your children regarding the ins and outs of your business, the better the chance they will understand what is required to operate it successfully and the kind of life that will result from those efforts.

EDUCATE

The earlier you get your kids involved in business, the more confident and successful they can become. Studies show that young entrepreneurs are typically more confident, creative and determined to achieve personal success than their peers. Starting a business, even a paper route, at a young age empowers children to come out of their comfort zones, sharpen their leadership skills and use their creativity to improve their businesses.

ACT

What are the things you wish you knew before you started a business? Now you have the opportunity to empower your child, teen or young adult with all the information, opportunities and skills you wish you had. You have the chance to help them learn from your mistakes and increase the likelihood they will achieve their dreams and taste the sweetness of success.

As human beings, we have short and selective memories. As soon as we are out of trouble, we tend to forget the trials and tribulations we had to endure before we emerged victorious. We are also impatient. It takes time and tremendous effort to build a business and it takes at least twenty years for a child to grow and mature into a responsible adult with the knowledge, ability and experience to run a business. But by raising them to develop the foundation and business skills, you are giving them the gift of potential and the clarity of a blazed trail. It's up to them to take it.

CHAPTER SEVEN

Step six

Evaluate Your FamilyPreneur Success

We've seen how important it is to instill in your children an appreciation for their familypreneur heritage, the basic skills they'll need to become successful, and the more specific business knowledge they'll use every day if they choose to follow in your footsteps. You have encouraged them to embrace the unique opportunity they have to not only become entrepreneurs but to build on the foundation of their family's hard work. You've slowly and carefully brought them into the business, allowing them to get their feet wet in different areas as they strive to discover what they love and what suits them. Now it's time to see how things are going. What's working and what's not? What are next steps?

In Chapter 6, I introduced the Small Business Checklist. I can't emphasize strongly enough the importance of doing regular periodic checks of the health of your business. Whether it's your basic financial performance, operations, your investments and resources, or your planning process, staying on top of these critical areas, quarterly, monthly, or even weekly, will help ensure that your hard work and energy is focused on the right areas at the right time.

Another area to pay close attention to that we haven't yet touched on is the market in which you operate – your competition.

YOUR COMPETITION

A friend of mine started a small software firm a number of years ago and was struggling to interest his teenage son in the business—until he was putting together a formal competitive analysis. Every business needs to create an initial competitive analysis prior to opening as part of the marketing plan, and periodically afterwards to keep up with market trends. My friend knew he needed someone to test out all of the software offered by his competitors. His son, who had no interest in sales, marketing, or even product development, jumped at the chance to see what was out there and report back to his father. It was a brilliant way for the son to become involved in the family business, but in a way that aligned with his interests. This is just another example of finding a way for your children to contribute, but on their terms. And what teenage boy would say no to more computer time? I'm going to briefly address the importance of competitive analyses here, because it is imperative that every business have an understanding of who and what they're up against in the market. If you haven't already done a formal comprehensive analysis, you should. If you have, I urge you to revisit and update it at least once each year and more, as necessary. In fact, most business owners are continually monitoring their competition. Your business is constantly changing, and so are your competitors. Your customers' needs, habits and tastes are changing as well and knowing who is doing what to address them and with how much success, will help you make the weekly or even daily decisions that determine your success.

A thorough competitive analysis will answer the following questions:

- Who are your competitors? How much market share do they have?

- What do they sell? How are their products or services differentiated from yours?

- What are their prices and how does their strategy differ from yours?

- What marketing techniques, channels, or strategies are they using?

- Where and how often are they advertising their product/service?

It's also wise to develop a SWOT analysis (strengths, weaknesses, opportunities and threats) for each of your competitors. You most likely wrote one for your own business plan, but developing one for each of your competitors can provide you with valuable insight that will further inform your thinking.

There are many ways, some obvious and some clever, to gather information about your competitors. Your children may be interested in helping with some or all of them.

1. INTERNET SEARCH

The first place to turn is your favorite Internet search engine. Search Engine Optimization (SEO) has become indispensable in enabling customers all over the world to find you (and your competitors). A simple Google search for any terms related to your product or service will show you who is successfully utilizing SEO and who isn't. If you aren't, you should be. Don't forget the competition's websites. Bookmark them and become a regular visitor.

2. SOCIAL MEDIA

Consumers, especially the younger ones, are now getting most of their information and news exclusively from social media. Sites like Facebook, YouTube, LinkedIn, Twitter, Instagram, and Snapchat, are just as, if not more important than any other marketing channel you have access to. Visit your competitor's pages and feeds often. Read and monitor their reviews, as well as your own, on sites like Yelp, Google Reviews and Trip Advisor.

3. TRADE ASSOCIATIONS, SHOWS AND CONFERENCES

Almost every product or service category has a trade group that serves as a resource for that particular industry and sponsors conferences or trade shows. Attend them regularly and don't be shy about networking with vendors, prospective customers, investors and yes, even competitors.

You never know where your next great idea may come from.

4. THIRD-PARTY SURVEYS

To gather specific information from your competition, you might consider utilizing any of the online survey services. By conducting a survey through email, you can gather intelligence about strategy, pricing, planning, and results that may not otherwise be readily available. Using a third party will encourage participation, as your competitors won't be eager to provide this information to you directly.

5. INDUSTRY ANALYSTS

Market research companies like Gartner and advocacy groups are a great resource for uncovering market trends and detailed performance and sales data depending on your industry.

6. FIRST HAND EXPERIENCE

Visit your competitors. There's no reason you, an employee, or a family member can't be a prospective customer to see firsthand how the competition does business. And don't forget to ask your customers, suppliers, and vendors about their experiences with others in your market niche. You never know what nuggets of information you might be able to gather from the people who have worked with your competitors. It's not sneaky; it's just common sense.

KEEPING PEACE AT WORK AND AT HOME

In your role as founder, partner, president, or boss, monitoring the success of your competition is a no-brainer. But as a parent, monitoring the progress of your children or other family members who work in your business can be...well, tricky.

There are obvious joys and benefits that come from working side by side with your children or other family members, but there are also pitfalls to avoid. As your child becomes integral in you business, many familypreneurs find they must go to great lengths to avoid the appearance of favoritism, giving special treatment, or fostering a culture in the workplace that may favor family over non-family. This is a difficult line to walk when loved ones are employees.

Below are some key issues that every familypreneur should be aware of:

GENERATION GAPS

In 2015, millennials became the largest generation in the U.S workforce[16] and it stands to reason the same holds true around the world. It is well documented that as a generation, millennials view work differently than the generations before them. Their expectations, work ethic, commitment level and attitude may clash with yours or the culture of your business. These conflicts

16 Millennials surpass Gen Xers as the largest generation in U.S. labor force, Richard Fry, Pew Research Center, http://www.pewresearch.org/fact-tank/2015/05/11/millennials-surpass-gen-xers-as-thelargest-generation-in-u-s-labor-force/

are not insurmountable but they may require communication, compromise and effort to find common ground, especially within the already emotionally charged relationship of a parent and child.

PERSONALITY CONFLICTS

Working closely with other people and personalities is complicated enough without the added layer of family baggage. Personality tests and psychometric measures have become common in larger companies to assess and categorize personality types and behavioral styles, helping employers better understand an employee's suitability for certain roles. Tests like the Myers-Briggs Type Indicator can open dialogue about differences in personality characteristics, how they affect behavior at work and dynamics that may occur in a group. Using these types of screening techniques may help avoid conflicts down the road.

UNEQUAL PAY

This seems to come up often but should be fairly simple to resolve. Family members should receive appropriate pay for the job they do, no more and no less. If you have three children working in the business, it might be tempting to pay them all the same salary. But if Suzie is the receptionist, and John is an accountant, they should be paid the market salary for their respective positions. It's logical that their pay is based on their contribution to the company, not on their relationship to you. Similarly, if a family member and a non-family employee have the same job and there is a noticeable difference in their pay, it may cause problems that could be easily avoided.

IN-LAWS

When children reach adulthood, their spouses may become candidates for joining the family business. Some business owners are reluctant to bring sons- or daughters-in-law into the fold, but they may have needed skills or experience that could benefit everyone involved. The in-laws are also likely to be involved in succession planning for the business so the benefits of including them may outweigh any potential risks.

POOR PERFORMANCE

In Chapter 2, I wrote about Thomas Edison and his children, including Thomas Jr. who attempted to work with his father in his laboratory. Edison called him "absolutely illiterate scientifically and otherwise." A scathing criticism from a father about his son for sure, but it illustrates the point that not every child is well suited to work in the family business. When performance or behavior issues arise, it is useful to apply a simple rule of thumb—"If the employee were not my child, what would I do?" Reprimanding your child in the workplace or terminating him or her is not easy, but it is necessary if the situation warrants it. Communicate openly and honestly with them, both at work and at home. The long-term family relationship is most important to preserve.

PERFORMANCE REVIEWS

If your business is large enough to conduct performance reviews, even informal ones, for your employees, you should for your kids or other family members as well.

To avoid favoritism and problems in the workplace, you should treat family members just as you would any employee—evaluating performance, rewarding success, and holding them accountable for failure. No one wants to intentionally hurt an employee's feelings especially when it's a family member. Avoiding the tough conversations though can have negative consequences on your business, other employees, or even relationships at home.

Laura Rosen, a certified public accountant with Sobel & Co. in New York, developed five steps to easing the evaluation process when family members are involved.17

1. Provide a written job description just as you would for any employee. This is the first and most basic step necessary to navigate along a career path.

2. Establish specific measurements for performance, using metrics that help the employee understand their own success and how they are contributing to the family business' success.

17 The Importance of Performance Evaluations for Family Businesses, Laura Rosen, CPA, Sobel & Co., LLC
http://sobel-cpa.com/sites/default/files/The%20Importance%20of%20Performance%20
Evaluations%20for%20Family%20Businesses-1.pdf

3. Determine what training will help the family member. To perform at peak levels, everyone needs access to the proper tools and resources.

4. Agree to meet regularly to track progress. Catching problems early can help mitigate end-of-year challenges that are more difficult to overcome once they have gotten out of hand. Feedback offered during these sessions must be reasonable and objective if they are going to make a positive impression and instigate cooperation and even change when necessary.

5. When changes do need to be made, collaborate and decide together how the family business member/employee can effectively implement the suggestions. Taking ownership over behavioral changes can lead to greater acceptance and commitment.

SUCCESSION PLANNING

Your hard-earned business isn't just a set of golden keys that you simply hand off to your children. It is a process that began in their childhood as you laid the groundwork for them to share and embrace the work you have made your passion.

If you have more than one child, you will have allowed them to gain experience in the business, explore their own interests and dreams, gather experience outside the business and the family, and determined what, if any, roles would be best suited for them, including leadership in the company after you have decided to step aside. Perhaps your daughter is a natural leader and a solid choice for president or CEO. Your son may have terrific business instincts but with interests elsewhere. He might be a wise choice to sit on the board of directors or serve in an advisory capacity. Another child may choose not to be involved at all, but maintain a small ownership stake.

It is tempting to provide equal ownership to all your children, but I would advise you to consider everything we've addressed in this book—ability, experience, desire, passion, and suitability when making those decisions. Most important to the long-term survival of your business is to have a plan that addresses ownership, governance and strategy after you have stepped away.

The experience of one family in Frankenmuth, Michigan provides a good lesson here. Frankenmuth is a small, tourist destination not far from Detroit. Main Street is lined with German restaurants, gift shops, and quaint arts and crafts stores—many of them owned by one entrepreneur who started with just one store in the 1970s, acquired other businesses, and eventually dominating the town. But when he passed away suddenly a few years ago, he had specified no succession plan. Responsibility fell to his widow, who had no interest in running the business. She and her children were forced to make critical decisions about the future of the shops and as a result, the future of the family's finances as well. A succession plan isn't just smart to have, it's imperative to ensure that your wishes for continuity of the business are realized and for the legacy you want to leave behind. If you don't already have the counsel of a trusted attorney, accountant or financial planner, you should have one to guide the development of a succession plan.

A well-crafted plan will address:

- The date you will step down and an outline of your involvement with the business going forward.

- The line of succession, including contingencies should anything happen to your designated successor(s).

- Specifics about the involvement of spouses.

- Detailed instructions and documentation of outstanding real estate leases and agreements.

Drafting this plan will also force you to think about the day you finally pass the baton to your child or children—the day your dream of independence and success officially bridges the generations. It is often difficult to let go. But those feelings will fade over time and become replaced with the pride for what you've built and passed along.

GIVING YOUR CHILDREN
MORE THAN JUST A BUSINESS

We have all seen it—the person stuck in a loveless job, putting in the hours out of duty or fear of doing something different, and without any passion or real interest. In the end, what we all hope for our children is that they choose the path that is right for them. You can provide the opportunities to learn your family business without the push to join. If you have inspired a passion and your child takes up the challenge, you will have a business capable of thriving throughout the next generation and beyond.

In the Eighties and Nineties, family businesses were still viewed as boring, obsolete, old-fashioned and lacking in innovation. Since the global financial crisis in 2008, we have seen the effects of profit maximization. The sustainable form of leadership that is commonplace in family businesses is now being viewed in a different, more positive light. Owners of family businesses are actually holding their companies in trust for their children and grandchildren. The values, beliefs and ambitions of the families behind these businesses are a driving force of sustainable value creation.

FamilyPreneurs feel a unique responsibility for future generations. One of the greatest challenges is the preservation of the family's unique culture and heritage, rooted in the values that are passed from generation to generation. It is from those values that our businesses thrive, our children find contentment and joy, our dreams are realized and we as individuals can feel the ultimate satisfaction of knowing what a significant contribution we have made.

CHAPTER EIGHT

Before
We
Part

My main goal in this book was to provide you with as much of that 20% of wisdom that yields an 80% return on your investment of time with the focus on growing an FamilyPreneur environment.My passion to help business owners like yourself continues beyond this book. To this end, I welcome you to get in touch with me through email at info@familypreneur.net.

My door is open for additional questions and support to help you realize the vision of both creating a vibrant business for your offspring and/or other family members, and, simultaneously, empowering those people, to consider the path of familypreneur. You can also visit my website at www.familypreneur.net to further explore ideas for your success.

Finally, if you liked this book—if it helped you even a little, please consider taking 5-15 minutes and writing a review, on Amazon, that shares what you felt was most beneficial for you. Reviews make a difference for authors and I greatly appreciate, In advance, your thoughtfulness in taking the time to offer this form of support. Meanwhile, here's to you, your family and your future. May it be all that you can dream it to be!

FAMILYPRENEUR:
THE SIX KEY STEPS TO RAISING
YOUR LITTLE ENTREPRENEURS

Every year thousands small businesses close their doors when the founder/owner is unable to continue due to multiple reasons; when these businesses cease to operate, they drag along the ways all values which were created over the years through hard work, dedication, perseverance and conviction.

Yet, these businesses could be saved and smoothly handed over to the siblings, relatives if the operating environment was set in prior years.

Every year, thousands of graduates hit the road looking for work, knocking on doors, hoping someone will give them a chance to prove themselves, gain experience and eventually build their wealth.

The truth is many of those graduates looking for work are walking away from Mom and Dad successful small business which is more than capable of providing that Dream Job!

As business owner, is Mom and Dad doing enough to increase the possibility of handing the reins to their siblings! Are Mom and Dad fully equipped with tools and technics to gradually introduce the kids to the business?

This book is for Mom and Dad business, gives the advices, guides and tools to manage their business therefore increasing the chances of keeping the family business alive and the jobs for life.

www.ingramcontent.com/pod-product-compliance
Lightning Source LLC
Chambersburg PA
CBHW071504210326
41597CB00018B/2684